St. Augustine
A to Z

St. Augustine A to Z

A Young Reader's Guide to America's Oldest City

Susan Shipe Calfee   Art by Oscar Senn

Wordwhittler Books
Ponte Vedra Beach, Florida

New edition with activities, published 2016

All rights reserved under International and Pan-American Copyright Conventions. No part of this book may be reproduced in whole or in part, in any form or in any manner without the prior written permission from the publisher at 3073 Cypress Creek Drive North, PonteVedra Beach, Florida 32082, or contact the author at www.susancalfee.com.

Book design and illustrations by Oscar Senn
Additional design by Frances Keiser

SUMMARY: A rhyming, educational ABC adventure book that explores St. Augustine, Florida's historical figures and landmarks, including a map and activity pages.

ISBN: 978-0-9895487-1-7 (soft cover)
ISBN: 978-0-9895487-2-4 (e-book)
ISBN: 978-0-9895487-3-1 (hardcover)
Library of Congress Control Number: 2013946247
Copyright: © 2013 by Susan Shipe Calfee

BISAC Subject Headings:
JNF025180 Juvenile nonfiction / history / US / state & local
JNF058000 Juvenile nonfiction / travel
JNF013010 Juvenile nonfiction /concept / alphabet

Available at local and online retailers or through:
WordwhittlerBooks.com

Wordwhittler Books
Ponte Vedra Beach, Florida

Printed and bound in USA

Acknowledgements

Special thanks to Lynn Skapyak Harlin, writer, editor and leader of the Shantyboat Writers Workshops, and to my shipmates who enriched every voyage.

Thanks to "A Gathering of Poets," Ann, Carolee, Mary Beth, Mary, Ria, Sharon and Yvonne for all we've shared over ten years of word whittling.

Thanks to illustrator Oscar Senn for getting it so right.

Loving gratitude beyond words to family and friends who've always said, "Of course you can." To my beloved late parents, my author-mother and dear father.

Dedicated to

*My dear grown-up children
Taylor and Chase
who love taking trips
all over the place.*

You're off to Great Places!
Today is your day!
You're off to Great Places!
You're off and away!
	—Dr. Suess

A
is for
ALPHABET

This one's new, what is it?
A book with St. Augustine's
famous places to visit.

B
is for
BASILICA
(Ba-SIL-i-ka)

Historic church, very pretty,
with paintings, music, a landmark
of our Oldest City.

C
is for
CASTILLO
(Kas-TEE-yo)

Go explore this old fort.
Its ancient iron cannons
defended the port.

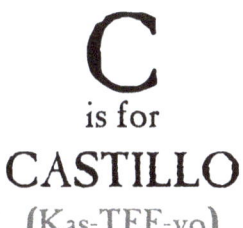

D
is for
DOUBLOON

Gold coins on a ship.
Join the pirates, find the treasure,
take a Black Raven trip.

E
is for
EGRET

Many birds fill the sky.
Seagulls and pelicans,
count them fly by.

F
is for
FLAGLER

A man who built trains,
and also the college
which carries his name.

G
is for
GHOST Tours

Scary stories at night.
Actors retell them
by old fashioned lamp light.

H
is for
HORSE and Carriage

See the sights while you ride.
Climb aboard where they line up
along the Bayside.

I
is for
INDIANS

The Timucua (Tee-MOO-kwa) lived here.
They had huts roofed with palm fronds,
went fishing with spears.

J is for
the Old JAIL

Don't be scared, take a friend.
Sit locked in a jail cell,
it's only pretend.

K
is for
KING Street
Find shops, museums and restaurants there.
Hear concerts, see shows
in the old town square.

L
is for
LIGHTHOUSE

Climb way up if you dare.
See its fun-filled museum,
take home memories to share.

M
is for
MENENDEZ
(Men-EN-dez)

Spanish conquistador (Kon-KEE-sta-dor),
who, in 1565, claimed the city
when his fleet reached these shores.

N is for NATURE

Find a park filled with flowers.
Or the farm full of gators,
there are shows by the hour.

O is for
OLDEST Schoolhouse

You must take a tour,
it's tiny and wooden.
Does it look like yours?

P
is for
PONCE DE LEON
(PON-seh DEH-leh-ON)

Great explorer from Spain.
He discovered Florida
and gave it its name.

Q is for Colonial QUARTER

People in costumes and settings that show how they lived, worked and dressed here, long, long ago.

R
is for
RIPLEY'S

Believe it or Not.
For strange, weird exhibits,
this is the spot.

S
is for
SIGHTSEEING

Do you enjoy it so far?
It lights up your mind
like seeing a star.

T
is for
TROLLEY

A ride you can take.
Step on and off
at the stops that they make.

U
is for
UNDER

The bright Florida sun.
At St. Augustine Beach
dig for shells, splash and run.

V
is for
VILLA Zorayda
(VEE-ya Zor-AY-da)

Made of shells and limestone
called Coquina (Ko-KEE-na),
it's still used for buildings and homes.

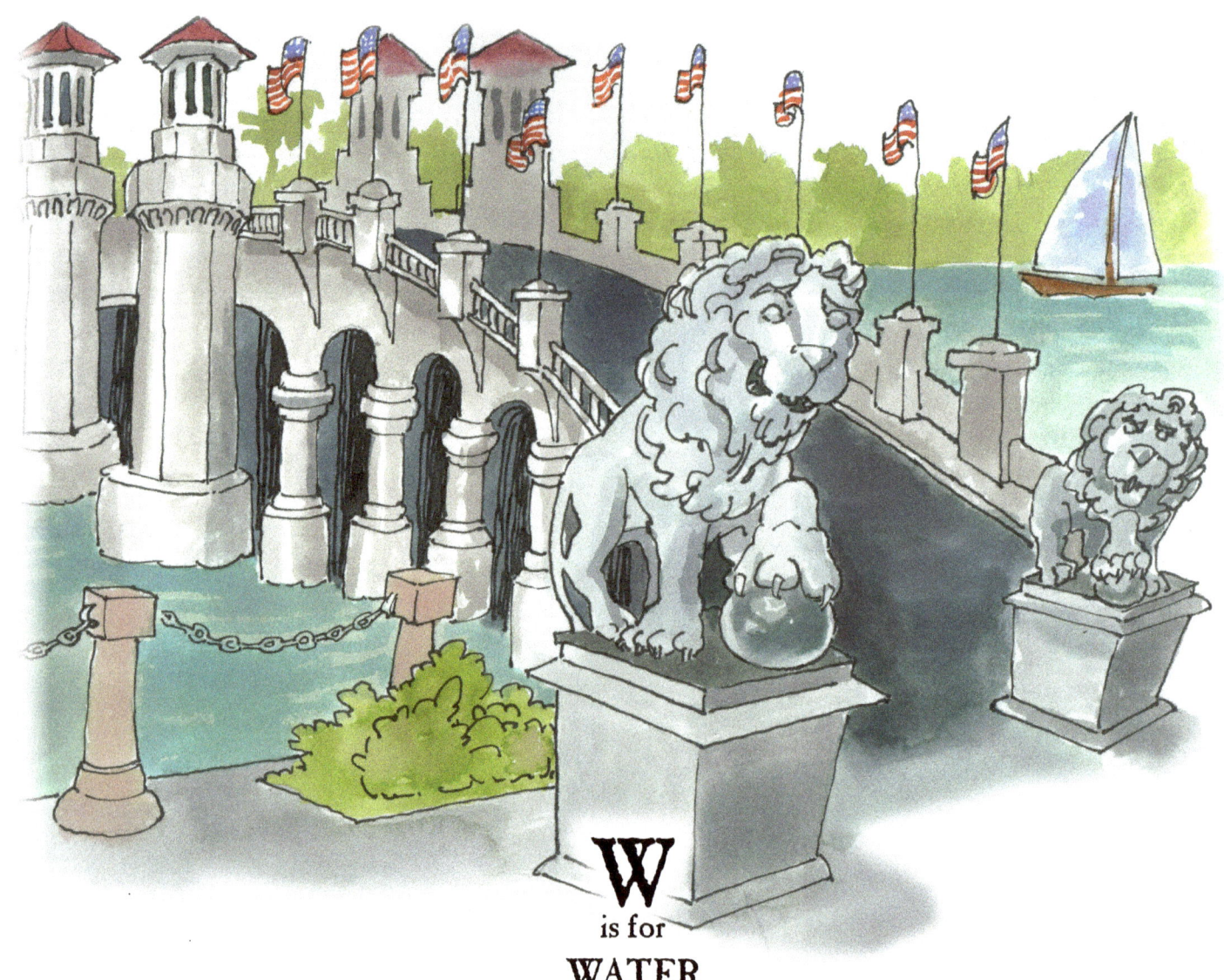

W
is for
WATER

There's so much around.
From the high Bridge of Lions
you see all over town.

X
is for
XIMENEZ-Fatio House
(HEE-men-ez FAY-shee-o)

A ship's captain, soldiers and artists stayed here
in this Boarding House
famous in long ago years.

Y is for

the Fountain of YOUTH

Go take a big drink.
Legend says you'll stay younger.
What do you think?

Z is for
ZOO
Where the crocodiles play.
See the Alligator Farm,
it's open each day.

St. Augustine A to Z

So much to learn and places to know.
Check the spots on this map, just where did you go?

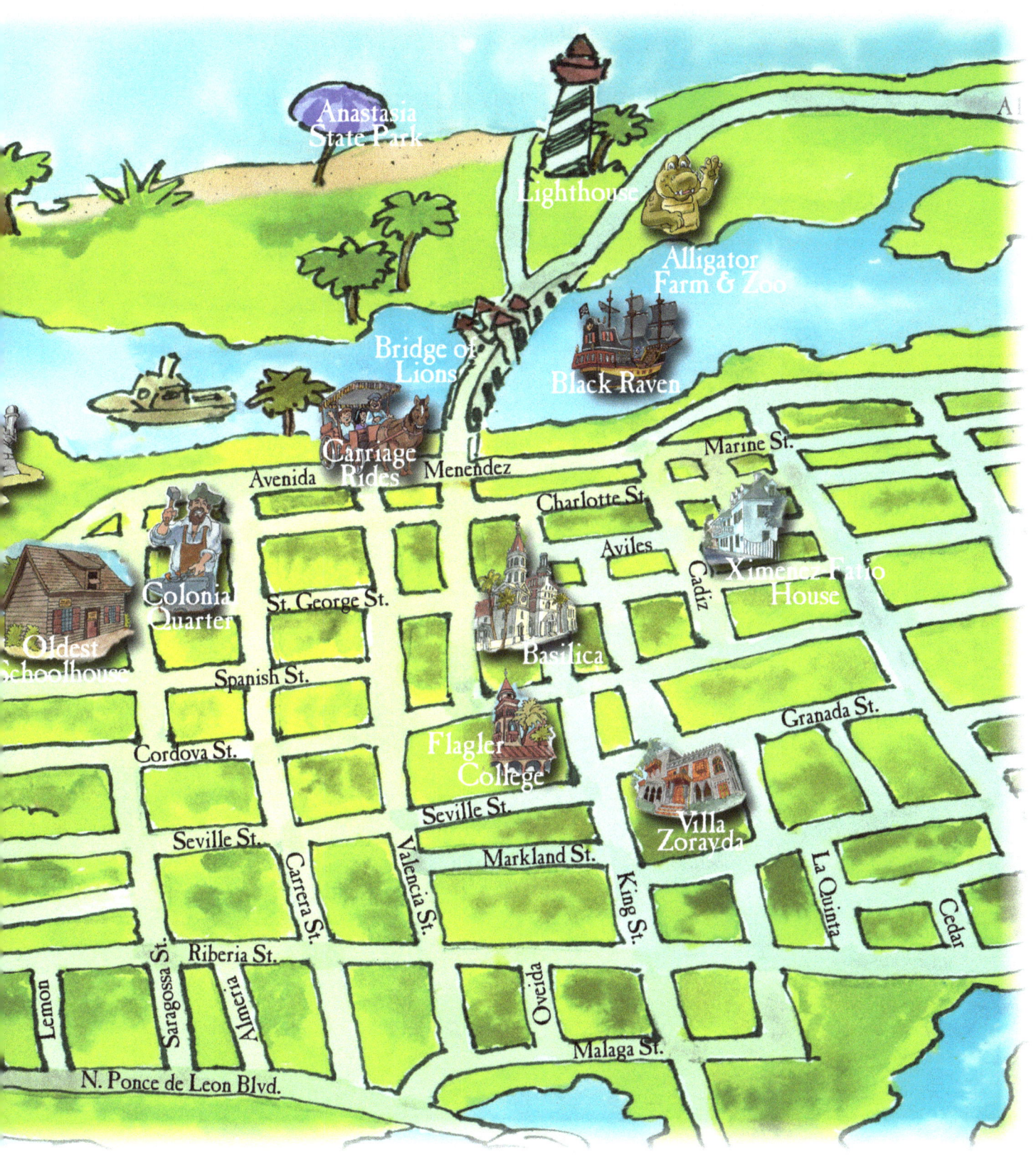

Do you have a favorite to share with a friend?
Keep this book and remember, please visit again.

I followed the map, and here's what I've seen.
I loved learning history in St. Augustine.

Maybe you found your own special places.
Practice writing them down, in their own special spaces.

RHYME TIME

Look in the book, don't skip a page.
You'll find same-sounding words, no matter your age!

Book, _____   Ride, _____

Fly, _____   See, _____

Man, _____   Star, _____

Old, _____   Stop, _____

Play, _____   Sun, _____

Hints: can/cold/far/fun/hide/hop/look/say/sky/tree

Make Up a Poem With a Rhyme of Your Own!

The title is the name of your poem. The author is the name of the person who writes it.

My Poem: _____
                                                                                                   Title

By: _____
                                                                                                  Author

_____
                                                                                                 Rhyme 1

_____
                                                                                                 Rhyme 1

_____
                                                                                                 Rhyme 2

_____
                                                                                                 Rhyme 2

_____
                                                                                                 Rhyme 3

_____
                                                                                                 Rhyme 3

More activities at www.SusanCalfee.com

MORE RHYMES

Try to make rhymes make sense. Be a poet!
Sometimes words fit together, before you know it.

City, _____		School, _____
Fort, _____		Share, _____
Gold, _____		Sound, _____
Guide, _____		Spain, _____
Learn, _____		Trip, _____

Hints: bold/fair/flip/fool/found/hide/kitty/plane/sport/turn

Make Up a Poem With a Rhyme of Your Own!

The title is the name of your poem. The author is the name of the person who writes it.

My Poem: _____
Title

By: _____
Author

_____
Rhyme 1

_____
Rhyme 1

_____
Rhyme 2

_____
Rhyme 2

_____
Rhyme 3

_____
Rhyme 3

More activities at www.SusanCalfee.com

Now you be an artist and color your way.
It's so much fun to try new things each day.
Add your rhymes, favorite places, go back, take a look.
Then put them together and make your own book!

About the Artist

Oscar Senn has been painting since second grade. His oil paintings are featured in collections all over the country.

He was educated at Ringling School of Art in Sarasota, Florida and has worked as an illustrator for the Jacksonville Times-Union and Miami Herald newspapers. As Art Director, he has worked for advertising agencies on both coasts. He has designed toys, TV commercials, posters, logos, annual reports, billboards and murals.

Oscar is the author of eight books for children, including **The Double Disappearance of Walter Fozbek**, and **A Circle In The Sea**. **Double Disappearance** was adapted for TV by CBS Storybreak. He has also illustrated many books by other authors.

He currently lives in Jacksonville, Florida with partner, Lori, a dog, four cats, and a turtle.

More of Oscar's work can be found at
www.oscarsenndesigns.com and www.oscarsennpaints.com

www.ingramcontent.com/pod-product-compliance
Lightning Source LLC
Chambersburg PA
CBHW040030091025
33786CB00058B/1827